REGIONS OF AMERICA

THE MID-ATLANTIC

NorwoodHouse Press

Francie Dolan

Cataloging-in-Publication Data

Names: Dolan, Francie.
Title: The Mid-Atlantic / Francie Dolan.
Description: Buffalo, NY : Norwood House Press, 2027. | Series: Regions of America | Includes glossary and index.
Identifiers: ISBN 9781978581166 (pbk.) | ISBN 9781978581173 (library bound) | ISBN 9781978581180 (ebook)
Subjects: LCSH: Middle Atlantic States--Juvenile literature.
Classification: LCC F106.D65 2027 | DDC 974--dc23

Published in 2027 by
Norwood House Press
2544 Clinton Street
Buffalo, NY 14224

Designer: Rhea Magaro
Editor: Tricia Hoffman

Photo credits: Cover, p. 1 Sergii Figurnyi/Shutterstock.com; p. 2 Tyler Bagwell/Shutterstock.com; p. 5 xbrchx/Shutterstock.com; p. 6 Five Buck Photos/Shutterstock.com; p. 7 Will eye/Shutterstock.com; p. 8 Jon Bilous/Shutterstock.com; p. 9 Dee Browning/Shutterstock.com; p. 10 Brian E Kushner/Shutterstock.com; p. 11 Jana Hacker/Shutterstock.com; p. 12 Stony River/Shutterstock.com; p. 13 F Armstrong Photography/Shutterstock.com; p. 14 Stockbym/Shutterstock.com; p. 15 tmpr/Shutterstock.com; p. 17 Ritu Manoj Jethani/Shutterstock.com; p. 18 StacieStauffSmith Photos/Shutterstock.com; p. 21 Vadim Rodnev/Shutterstock.com;

Printed in the United States of America

TABLE OF CONTENTS

WHERE IS THE MID-ATLANTIC?

The Mid-Atlantic is a **region** of the United States. It has seven states. It also includes the District of Columbia.

The Mid-Atlantic

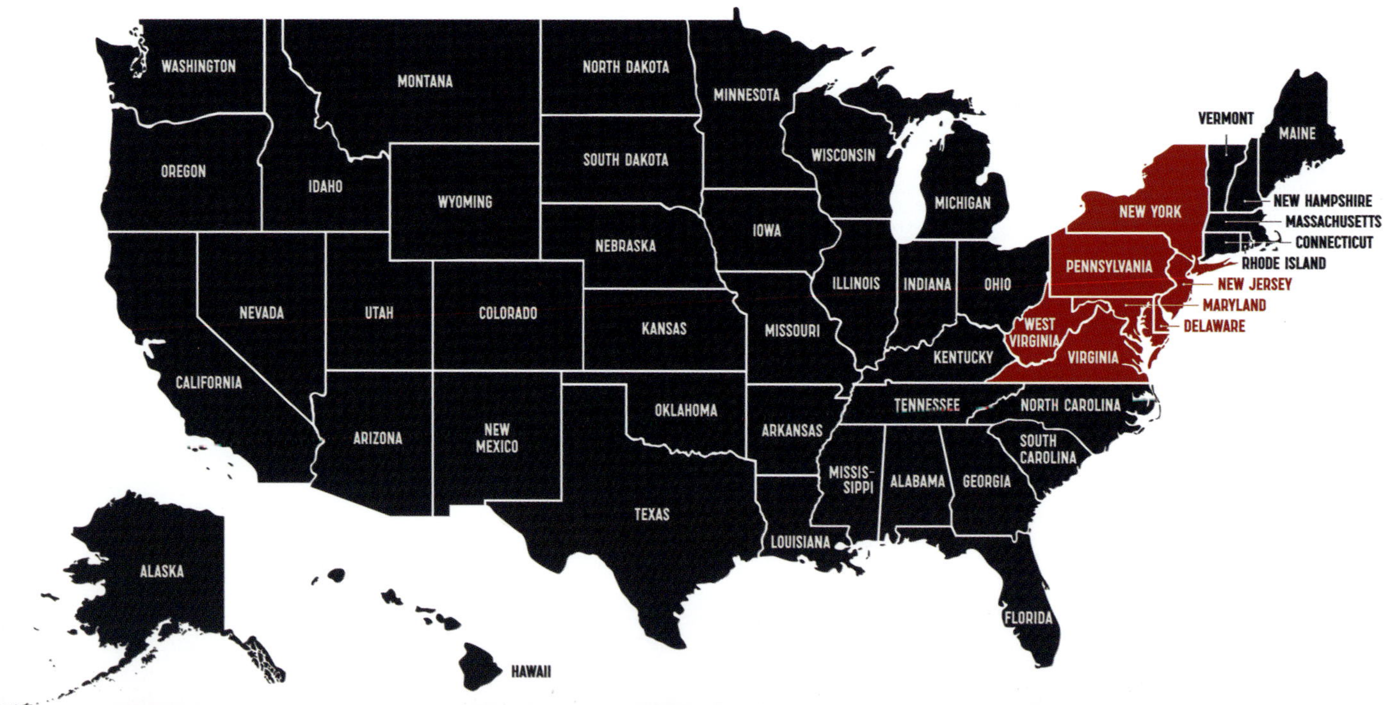

THE LAND

The Mid-Atlantic is in the northeast. All the states, except Pennsylvania and West Virginia, border the Atlantic Ocean. These states form some of the middle of the country's **coastline**. That's what gives the region its name.

There are four **distinct** seasons. Summers are warm to hot. Winters are cool to cold.

Parts of the Appalachian Mountains run through the region. They include the Blue Ridge and Allegheny Mountains.

The land between the mountains and the ocean has **fertile** soil. It is good for growing cotton, peaches, corn, and other crops.

A **network** of waterways connects to the ocean. The Delaware River flows for more than 300 miles (483 kilometers). Chesapeake Bay is the country's largest **estuary**.

Delaware River

Chesapeake Bay

THE PEOPLE

Indigenous people once lived across the region. Some tribes were the Lenape and Piscataway.

Today, many people live in small towns.
Some work on farms and fishing boats.

Many people live in **urban** areas. New York City, New York, is the largest city in America.

Washington, D.C., is the nation's capital. It is in the District of Columbia. Many people who live there work in the **federal** government.

THINGS TO SEE AND DO

You can visit the National Aquarium in Baltimore, Maryland. It is home to thousands of **marine** animals.

SHORE HERO
Project Green Teens
Plastic Trash Busters

In Virginia, you can tour Colonial Williamsburg. It is the world's largest living history museum. Actors show what life was like in the 1700s.

You can board *Maid of the Mist* to take a boat ride under Niagara Falls. It is the largest waterfall in North America. It is between New York and Canada.

GLOSSARY

coastline (KOHST-line): the place where the land and the ocean meet; the outline of the coast

distinct (di-STINGKT): different from the rest; easy to tell apart from others

estuary (ES-choo-er-ee): the wide part of a river where it joins the ocean

federal (FED-ur-uhl): having to do with the government of an entire country; the national government of the United States

fertile (FUR-tuhl): good for growing; rich and full of nutrients

Indigenous (in-DI-juh-nuhs): the earliest known people to live in a place

marine (muh-REEN): of or having to do with the ocean

GLOSSARY

coastline (KOHST-line): the place where the land and the ocean meet; the outline of the coast

distinct (di-STINGKT): different from the rest; easy to tell apart from others

estuary (ES-choo-er-ee): the wide part of a river where it joins the ocean

federal (FED-ur-uhl): having to do with the government of an entire country; the national government of the United States

fertile (FUR-tuhl): good for growing; rich and full of nutrients

Indigenous (in-DI-juh-nuhs): the earliest known people to live in a place

marine (muh-REEN): of or having to do with the ocean

network (NET-wurk): a large number of things that cross over each other or are connected to each other

region (REE-juhn): an area or territory; part of a country

urban (UR-buhn): having to do with cities and city life

THINKING QUESTIONS

1. How does the name *Mid-Atlantic* describe the location of the region?

2. Which Mid-Atlantic states touch the Atlantic Ocean? Which don't?

3. Name a big city in the Mid-Atlantic.

4. Name one Native American tribe from the Mid-Atlantic.

5. What is Colonial Williamsburg?

INDEX

ABOUT THE AUTHOR

Francie Dolan is a writer from Seattle, Washington. She loves American history and trivia. It is her goal to travel to all 50 states, visit their capital cities, and eat a special food from each place.